The Sower

by Marc Darnell

Cyberwit.net
HIG 45 Kaushambi Kunj, Kalindipuram
Allahabad - 211011 (U.P.) India
http://www.cyberwit.net
Tel: +(91) 9415091004
E-mail: info@cyberwit.net

Contents

Dark Matters

Unclose yourself, look— the day's on fire,
shadows that are soothing being consumed,
roses safe as buds forced to bloom—
how harsh the light the seas of stars expire,

how little time their distant rays require
to stoke an incandescence out of room.
Forget light's good intentions, don't assume
all glow is good, the lumen's getting higher.

Beware— lightning bugs that burn the air
with blinks that have a sting for every watt
now boil up the ebon reserves of skull.

Night was first, it came with black to spare,
and fostered mystery, not knowing what
was in the dark and irresistible.

Bedside Manner

According to my heart you are
perfect, but science says something weaves
nighted cells that never leave
your bones alone. Still you were

my wing when I was clipped, unsure
of everything. You tossed my book
to break my gaze, a serum when I looked
in those infective eyes. No tumor

could survive you, let alone this coward
in your blood, so nurse the whirl
of life that stays when chemicals have left

you cringing to noise. I won't say a word,
holding the hand of one pinned by the world
for now, who's full of love and so much lift.

CO$_2$

See, oh, two
oxygens per molecule,
please don't ridicule—
I thought it one
for this carbonic
acid gas
that from tonic
waters pass,
or residue
of respiration.

See, oh,
carbon mono,
a sister oxy-
molecule
I've confused—
the toxic
breathless breath
(though this an oxy-
moron be)
of used
fossil fuel,
coal and oil
destructive distillation,
one atom nearer thee
to death.

The Sower

Raised on lukewarm milk and bread,
all my corn-pone peers are dead.
I'm the last of the pasture poets,
unpasteurized.

I'm unrefined and not as good
as Frost or cummings, almost mad
from too much Roethke, (who is Yeats?)
but civilized.

I walked in realms beyond the sheds,
suntan-scarred and porkchop-fed
from fattened runts Dad raised as pets,
euthanized.

Swayed as grass I often led
a slanted life without a shred
of bravery— I let life get
italicized.

Find the seeds in things I've said—
germinating, never read.
My time is past, but princes wait,
unrealized.

Pink Baby On Yellow Bed Sheets

And the world outside screams and swirls,
but the room celebrates its own cubism,
drapes angular, aquamarine,
protective of the Jesus girl,
clementines in a chain
off the corner of the dresser.

Light rolls in a seagull fog
upon the sleeping
bulb of rosiness.

O nesting blank, amoebic,
you are all globular and dream
with eddying thoughts of
your mother's waning spring.

But beyond this Cezannian roof
of sweat and crooked straw,
the crowds cut each other endlessly,
revising their laws
and dying dumber than they were born.

The Silver Lark

She plays the flute in a house in the country,
not letting others hear her play; she is
very good, quite exceptional, practicing her
chromatic scale that bends upward to the sky
as the pear and cherry trees bend in with
dying autumn ears. The attic is a cathedral
where notes of the E-flat scale ricochet back
to the gleam of the flute. When she plays a
quick skipping song, birds become envious,
listening through the shingles– *this human,*
this soft doll, with her brittle wand, better
at what we were born to do, can she fly also?

She is beckoning a faun to come out of
the withering thicket by the creek, or some
new romantic beast from out of unharvested
cornfields, some translucent prince to follow
the music up the unpainted steps to her cold,
pyramidical, raftered room and recline till
all codas have completed. She wants sprites
to weep, her tremolo to pulse through stone
down to underground rills. The unmowed
grass quivers and bends toward the house
despite the wind– her graminaceous arena,
as she aims for high G beyond the sky.

His Tinnitus

Piccolos satanic,
tsetse screams,
some compete—
a shout of bees
drowning out
life's intricacies.
O cry of gnat,
whimper of newt,
tap of tine,
gnash of earwig,
scrape of egg,
chalkboard-speak.

Some crackle or hum
in tainted keys
or different degrees
of rat-a-tat drum.
Ringings eat
with scintillating
no one sees.
Tubular tolling
does not cease.

One insectile
soprano a day
joins this viral,
aural plague.
Sirens are keen
to call his hoarhead

home sweet home
and dance and ting.
He doesn't ask
why or for whom
they ring, or if
they follow at death,
but only if
they're heard by the deaf.

Hopes And Preyers

Some uncage the itch inside
by sinking into children's cheeks—
men who lie before they speak
and smile as if there's nothing wrong.
Layered clothes won't shield the young
from serpents fond of skin, and drunk
on disappointments, satisfied
by black and blue and household rank.

The cowardly prefer to hide,
then pull the shades and clip the boys
flown above the fringe of fright.
The shiest and naive deliver
pleasure sought without a noise.
The weakest hurt the most, forever.

Inertia

I was anchored
as you strewed

your love around
this heart you found,

but you were
a reckless blur,

unpinned, not settling for static.
My love for

you was timeless, yours
was sorely too athletic.

Inheritance

My fear of living is genetic—
father all hammer on the roof, afraid
to even laugh with us beneath, and mother frantic
to keep his bed aligned and made,

always staring at neighbors while she talked
in short, complaining sentences, but questioning
nothing. Their long gone passivity still marks
all my life's unfurling

hesitations— a branding that's prodded me toward
bouts of ironclad seclusion,
each day guarding my crystalline heart,
but never learning that isolation

gives partial protection from everything,
but promises the passing down of nothing.

OCD

Perfection's his shtick—
excessive checks, reps, tics

that tie his noose.
He sees inanimates to be fixed—

a jar's lid loose,
a light switch off, but maybe

not completely.
Such an Eden can't be,

so he dreads dirty, lonely days,
remotes with fingerprints,

and the scourge of lint.

On A Limb

I am a leg— my musculature refines
how hard I kick. Thigh and I have always
debated his inclusion in what defines
me down to the heel of life, and I don't sway,

stubborn clear to my stub-borne end oh
blood be still— coagulate on the terms
I may require you for any innuendo,
no matter how trite the scarification, or burns

scribed in skin. I skip where children hop-
scotch, and fly like Hermes, tendon single-winged.
Would amputation be liberation, stop
the torso in its tracks? I feel unhinged,

as though severed, my phantom limb replacement
getting all glory, pomp and accomplishment.

Passenger Seat

The year went very well
without you at the wheel.
Months of Google searches
found a sliver of truth,
packaged to be purchased.
A feverish week defeated
A, B, and type C flu
as happy days completed
your one-act tragedy.
Happier hours retrieved
poems you swore you threw,
and, on closer inspection,
they weren't written by you.
Minutes curtly finished
your Mahlerian symphony,
and thirteen dragging seconds,
with half a cigarette,
revised your tired, syrupy
autobiography
with only minor regrets.
For just one year without you,
it certainly was an endeavor,
but you were always timeless,
time's underachiever.

Proof

Around you why do I feel juvenile,
construction of my reasoning unbuilt?
I love you, let me tell you how I know:

I slept and drew your face, oh long the mile
it was to track your impulses, they wilt
away my wile, my want, I know not how.

Ravenous

The cancer in her head was like a shroud,
communication was to no avail.
The gray was not transmitting as it should—
an interference from a tainted veil.

The woman's heart knew beating, there was no
problem of involuntary reflex,
and breathing still had portion of control—
the stubborn soul was slowly going next.

Unable to embrace or show her humor
the way she did when she was thirty-five,
her love and lust were dead, the clever tumor
strangled nerves, no memory could survive

a thing with such a motive and maneuver,
so hungry as it swallowed her surrender.

Rockabye

Combat killed all calm in him,
leaving gray faces and specters
of boys he killed, their splayed limbs.
With snare-drummed ears he hears
nightly SOS's that trigger fear.
This is the graze of bulleting war.

Discharged, he prays for a tumor—
light on the brain, a sheath
of ardor so graceful it clears
all horrors, singing him to sleep forever,
a compassionate abduction by death—
not ratatat repetitions of gore,
a truce with life, and what a departure,
no more memorial torture.

Runt (Seen But Not Heard)

I was slight, surrendering all power
to those who proved more powerful than I.
They had it all, a staunch reality
that I could not compete with by the hour.

My strength lay in my silence, now turned sour—
too much noise broke my monotony
which crumbled soon my proud sobriety—
before intelligence my calm wits cower.

I am nothing all the someones prove,
yet to nothing I shall not return—
unremarkable flesh still leaves its mark—

conscience from its origin does not move.
Even in its shame the soul won't burn,
and I'm not my own failure in the dark.

Gogh

He cuts with carnal hues, tears
tints to bits in tongued strokes

as granulated heaven sears
a twined landscape full of streaks

to snare the meteorite, the too
albino bloom or aster trail

in ripened rainbow, savage to
the tamest eye. Spiral hail

contorts stars, as brittle auras
cake and clot the air, hazes

bruise in indigo and melt the
crust that fogs all eyes, sunrises

leap with amber teeth to peel
retinas. He whips the sky

without the urge to illustrate,
but coat the void, then reveal

the god behind a shard of light

The Active Boy

Cracking eggs, his mother shouts he does
nothing that's of any worth or substance,
and that he thinks too much about applause
from things he'll never do— *oh just for once,*

go play a sport, stop scribbling down emotions—
that stupid dream of music and the arts!
He wants to show a little man's intrusions
into a grown-up world, the scary parts

like every Sunday seeing Daddy throw
his fist at her, those raw humiliations—
things he first saw Bugs or Elmer do,
but conks with ripping bumps of more duration.

If only he'd go kick a ball around
he wouldn't see her falling to the ground.

Untranslatable

Depression is a relative of death—
the slipping of the psyche to another
strata, down to where your pump and breath
are never welcome— not purgatory, but rather

a kingdom of ennui not black but shaded.
The ones of highest health will tell you not
to worry— that you momentarily faded
with that error in your skull— that blot

of badness on your blued brain— misfired
messages that never seem complete,
so you aspire to be: No Assembly Required,
and difficult a life that makes you delete

those who say it's easy, whom you damage,
who fear your pain and never decipher its language.

The Poet Revises His Revision

You have no flair with pen in hand—
get off the throne, your wit lacks weight.
You're programmed to impress, and hesitate
to fix a phrase you now don't understand.

True genii should reprimand
your enigmatic hand, affix your rate
of pomp and pay. Of late,
you only flair with mirror in hand,

a cock who jots a junked dialect.
Brilliance has no patience for the thick,
you crow, *it doesn't wait,* but it's too late

for you, with thoughts you fail to resurrect,
and arrogance marks *you* thick
when it dictates what you do and don't delete.

Evaporation

If you're the sun, then I'm the rain.
I hit the ground without color—
your amber lifts till I'm in air again.
I dampen skin with deep dolor—
you dry me up so people grip
the earth with warm toes and never slip.
I come in waves, chaos out of spite,
dreading your broom of burn, I might
end this now, I'm only meant
for wet brood and cold sulk at night.
Complete your arc, your coy descent
and dry my tears from this cement.

Linen Castes

Segregate the towels and the sheets,
the colors and the whites, and start their cycles,
colors are on 6, whites on 3—
exclude all reds, or else you're in a pickle—

they will bleed and leave their crimson stains,
so all the maids will flinch when making beds,
and they don't need more Honeymoon Suite complaints,
thus make a separate cauldron for the reds.

If the Mother Washer fails to spin
wring and take them to The Whipping Tree,
or else the maids will scream, unseam your skin
as laundry Mangler folds you to a T.

Mother

I was one who thought that motherhood
took little skill, a secondary world,
but it was first to her, and so it stood,
and she was first to me. Now I grow old,
recalling things she did that made me bold—
those bare and veining hands took battled pans
off war-torn stoves, uncuffed the pasted cold
from little wrists that ached erecting snowmen.

I saw, a soldier home from kindergarten,
her paisley sleeveless shirt on browning arms,
the small-pox vaccination scar. I'm certain
it was my moon, and she was every star.
She was the only god in this child's eyes.
These memories still make me fall and rise.

Note To Self

Sense the world— it seems an easy mission,
deciphering it in rhyme and meter,
just don't be vulgar, that's amateur,
so euphemize carefully in revisions,

though it's chic in limerick submissions,
but you'll never be a star, you're amateur—
without panache, just lumpy lines with meter,
though rhythms of your heart don't need revision,

so write them like drums when earth is still—
end bitter thoughts and finding fault
in those with less artistic sense

who never *get* your poems, but still,
you speak them from the heart, it's not your fault
to you they make a world of sense.

Recital For One

If I could have stood back and heard myself
play those subdued, tumbling notes on yellowed
and untuned ivory keys, constructing chord
and mellow discord, I might have found belief

in myself earlier. All I knew was life
as a ten-year-old, never knowing how hard
it'd be years later to make music from words,
but it seemed easier then during those brief

summers of first poetic attempts. Behind
me sat my tragically shy father with his
newspaper lowered, in what I saw as bliss,

liking something he heard. Afraid to be kind,
his presence was his music to me, and this
made me love him more and judge him less.

To Daughters Not Mine

(for Minny and Gracy)

I'll look for trolls around you
and check the ground beneath,
cornering those that want you,
removing all their teeth.

Try not to fear the dark—
it only leads to more.
The two of you may talk—
I'll slightly crack the door.

Rise and twirl to school
with sunless hands so small.
Laugh and don't be fooled
away from feeling tall.

Fall in love with books
before a prince and palace.
Yes, the rabbit talks—
stay as close to Alice.

Play when you are old
and dance when you are sick.
It's good to flee the fold
when people get too thick.

The years will quickly move—
a rushing life regrets,
so tell the ones you love
before the heart forgets.

13 ways of using a blackbird

(after reading Wallace Stevens's poem
"Thirteen Ways of Looking at a Blackbird")

1

blackbird singing in the dead of night
sings for the dead
who thought they'd be flying by now

2

in death you will dust away our simian flecks
from desks and precambrian paperweights
our skin cells imprinting like ducklings on
all the love and black you are

3

the blackbird soars scans for molesters
and takes down their names
as if imps who whisper in study hall
detention awaits to castrate

4

the blackbird is plucked till a runted chicken
not eaten but stretched for slapstickin'

5

running out of virgins for the dragon
they stoned the blackbird for good crop yield

6

fly petite velociraptor evolver to sky
alert all ornithurines man mutates even faster

7

leaving one grin of a feather behind
it was just a sloth that flew
now hunted for all the horror it soared over

8

four and twenty blackbirds
baked in a pie
leave the witch's oven unfit for children

9

closer crow-magnon
eat from our hands o onyx cock
as we loop your neck with an albatross

10

children are beaten
it is the blackbird's fault
the ozone is scratched

the blackbird's fault
there is ache
the blackbird

11

o oiled oracle show us
the black that is darker than black
is that where the devil hides in inked quills?

12

the cherry tree is full of blackbirds
coal-ripe fruit that pulls at the pits in our eyes
and at the obsidians of the gravel path
balance us forever

13

from the air the silo is spinning
the blackbird must be circling
straw-boned hypnotist we sleep already

coal

some live love their life human
but I am bitumen
burning
without bodily yearning
distilling
but killing
the air

I have no fear
being bitumen
is perfect inhuman
and fossil fuel tells no lies to anyone

in stoves and in hell
I am orange heaven

diamond is coal's rare imago
given
luster and show
I want to be diamond so

oh coal is moved
great distances and secretly loved
my death is quick
whereas humans just get sick

in the end I'm burned
not boxed buried or urned
and to smoke I shall return

Don't Tell Them Yet

(for Minny and Gracy)

When the daughters twirl
in the yard of fireflies
and ask in the waning light
why Molly the white
German shepherd has been gone
for days and days,
one shouldn't announce dead on
she died and suffered long,
but that she's after butterflies.

Dancing life since birth,
these remarkable gems
don't know death, the why,
the take-away of earth.
They shouldn't know as night unfurls
the dog is lost forever to them
or lying in a near field to die.
Say the pet's return to the girls
is always a possibility.

Don't intrude upon naivety
or dash that hope in their lives,
giving them cause to ruminate—
the young must never meditate
or be told *oh, there will be other pets.*
They don't need mortality yet
to taint a mentality

we long to retrieve ourselves,
nor hurt their heart's duality
to sometimes remember and often forget
that pets do die,
but the missing ones chase the butterfly.

God As An Iconic Toy

In that room is a red ball
with no key to open the door,
and it's impossible to peek.
There's always been a ball in that room,
even before we knew it was there.

People communed and decided
it was red, round and bouncy
without seeing it.
Groups argue if it is really red
and just how high it can bounce.

We are dumb to the ball.
That is one smart ball.
When you die, the love part of you
passes through the closed door
where you dance around the ball with others,
but don't whisper bad things about it.

It might sit there content,
or spin with wrath.
It says it isn't hell,
but it has a hell of a bounce.

You're lucky the ball will have you,
so thank it, then smile and shut up.
You're going to love everybody else in there,
even if you hated them before.
Get used to the room, to the ball,
get used to it now before you see it.

I Am Rodin

I have a warehouse of boulders
I've been chiseling into statues—
some of butter, easy to carve with
a big fat spoon, others of mica,
which if I rush with a circular saw
end up a hill of flakes. The hardest
to chisel are diamonds with such
hope of becoming staples in the
art world, but sometimes I don't
even start on those, texting Atlas
to drop what he's holding and put
them back in the stars. I turn
the boulders into people who are
sad, or tall thin stalks of me with
issues. I smooth them and perfect
them according to what I think is
perfection. When I let in the statue
experts, some who can't even sculpt
with any complexity, and dummies
who wander into the warehouse with
their phones and crudity and a snot
view of the world, the experts remark,
But what do the statues mean? and
I answer— a practiced answer, *Did*
Picasso stand by his paintings and
explain them? They ask, *Are you*
comparing yourself to Picasso? As
my self-confidence is below thirty
percent that day, I say, *Let's go with*

that. When the dummies ask what
they mean, I don't know if they are
talking to me or their phones. I try
not to give a stuffy answer, and
pretend I hear the dock buzzer to
let in another order of boulders.

Morph

I became my poem—
snared in its essence,
or the essence I assumed
I put there,
thinking of nothing more
than a life of literary presence,
but each metaphor was a crumb
that did not stick.
It pulled me toward
its nonsense center, its archaic
adjectives and phrases
till I became the words,
the patsy curls of the esses,
then the PC's electric ink,
leaving behind my arrogant stink
from writing fluffy essays
and never being unique
or muse-inspired—
a pen unfired.

There I was
in flickering stanzas,
an anonymous, unsent file,
reduced to the most
clownish of serious styles—
Comic Sans MS—
italicized, never to stand erect
with any academic respect,
bound to fall off the margin, lost
in a font so frivolous,
soon wiped by a virus.

my bell jar

I'll give you a nice bell
me inside I didn't place
the glass around I more
humanely would have
used a porous element
so I still politely breathe
beyond the fifty years
I choke at now vacuum-
packed and freeze-dried

I didn't mind the womb
it was opaque and I was
obsessively guarded by
the only one who ever
loved me but this glass
cruel everyone sees me
mourn trip tremble bang
they point hear nothing

I'm endlessly vocalizing
I thought it was crooning
but no a life death mating
scream the worst of glass
is seeing prettier people
exhale twirl laugh beside
lovers touching tossing
unshattered children in
the autumn evening air
beneath strings of lights

orange purple I remain
guilty chaste confused
gray within this grave

I believe the rip gape twist
of god will be done soon
o *believe* what an empty
verb I'm a damp pouch
with a soul that traveled
nowhere we are tearing
contraptions wanting to be
more than chemical thank
you last O_2 molecule thank
you last ray thank you all

obituary for a calendar

it had its
latticed lifespan on
the wall
though it held an extra
two months
miniaturized
on the ass of
December
as a plea of
survival to 2019

the neon highlighter
slashed it date
by date yet it
kept its diptych panache

march an airbrushed
waterfall
april a poisonous frog
may a gash of petunias

we had tacked it
on an unclean wall
crucifying it
then standing
around as it
bled its staled
31's away

and we wanted its
gridded judgmental
face over with
that held 4 seasons
of our parenthetical
(dirty secrets)
our gouged-out
ambitions ###
and asterisked
failures ***

obituary for a credit card

they called you Visa
but I called you Lover

16-digit magic man
you fed me when
your dirty brother
debit card
deserted me

someone stole your
heart abused you down
to negative 399 dollars

I went years without you
wheezing powerless
but you came back to me
a polyvinyl boomerang
with me now
my rectangular amour

but I give pieces of you
away till you are
near zero but still I keep
you at my butt cheek
pressed and arched
when I squat
desperately for pennies

I extract you
from my wallet
with your pulsing
hologram hawk your
plasticity and potential
so stoic erect
so plumped to take
my wishful charge

then you expired—
a crib death in my wallet
and the stork never brought
your offspring

obituary for a house

it was old
even when built
leaking at the panes

but the children were
grateful for those drafts
on humid nights when

it could not cool itself
from the coals of day
and though it became brittle

in serest winter it never
broke or chaffed away
and all its boxiness

had a soul of a father
for the mother in it
who had no husband

this house held her
in its cubicle love
when no man would

stay more than a night
and it saw her children
to school with its

browed eaves and window
agape with each departure
but all the children are

now gone the mother
too and a house not
lived in is not alive

obituary — lily

we strode by
our briefcase pace

till the woman
snipped you for a

slow sill death
who are we so alive

we sever things
to show prowess

with sharp objects?
a bouquet of you is

genocide a hate
crime for an

orange quivering
star of a mouth

obituary for a poet

he wrote doomy
dire poems
passed over
by nouveau
optimistic editors

then he stopped to
marry chained to a
cutlass and a shack
of fat spawns
raised on
processed food
who never finished
community college

at fifty-four he tried
once more writing
this time cramming
light into the poems
and taking out
the dark but all
the forced-in hope
was a virus
attacking his honesty

consumed by belly
and bbq by erectile
failure by his slow
palsy in the mirror

he died on a blank
untitled white bed
while his wife
wrapped china
with his poems
(original copies)

obituary for a tattoo

seamed into forearm
twenty years past
it went from crisp
licorice scorpion to
blue blued
arachnidian smear
claws of fuzz
benign no emblem
of rebellion

the skin aged
crinkled till
its whip sting was
only a question mark

fade me too
like ink
bleed me into the world
I was unwillingly
injected and
dissipate

obituary for a tornado

we will cherish
the 33 minutes
he had on earth
axled out of the sky
in the devil heat
of early spring an
ess butter knife

May baby, a Taurus
bull-strong for his age
a constant feeder
not letting go of
the earth's bosom
unless to wail
like an ogre infant

a prodigy
he threw a house high
and turned a pond
to a cattail chaos
with a floating
drowned calf

he carved with
his alpha whip
crop circles
drove hay strands
into elms but
broke no glass not

one pane of the
greenhouse
not a bull after all

prozac 80 mg

I feel fiend and fire
the under wants to play
no light this hour
best it stay this way
this night should never day

dark matter with such assault
air gone
leaving my lungs a vault
that cedes its space to clay
I don't miss the sun
or a hair of sky
this night should never day

I squint at graves
and burrow through mud till
there comes still
then shrieks in waves
with waves of all
my blood I drew
been here forever tomorrow
this night should never day

I trod the moor
fear others and for
others like me
sleeping themselves away
till they wake to this
till they wake this

no urge to pray
this night should never day

fetal on salted ground
eaten not found
my heart palpitating prey
I didn't want to live die this way
this night should never day

ruffled bedsheets resembling a corpse

walk the halls
try not to smell
these are people
who've lived
longer respect
them oh room
109 died today
wait until the
relatives leave
strip the bed
put the twisted
S of a bedsheet
in a bag with
the faded shit-
stained gown
wear gloves for
any c-diff
contamination
dust kill germs
high to low
this is the last
window she
looked out
the tv remote
fell from her
hand that's how
they knew wipe
the gray hairs
from the shower

drain fold the
toilet paper to
a V erase her
life high to low

the asshole orderly

get off me
dusty fart
I'll never be
old like you
just wheeze
that crotchety
way you do
I came to clean
you seizure
not to carry you
to the can
your skin it rips
like husks I had
an iguana like
you but I'm a
rubber man
with rubbers man
bouncer of beds
your call button
jams the link
the ice clink
of my boo's
cold texts
you're deadbook
friended when
dumped here
so play yahtzee
it's real easy
with parkinson's

roll a die and die
wheel this hell
forever I'll never
pickle here I'm a
smooth-skinned
suave stag
going home to a
squeeze on the
vine every night
this job's fluff
my shift's up

the astronaut has racing thoughts

I thought I
knew ennui
on the 8 billion-
bodied ground—
no wife child
no friends to
tell of my dense
heart the gravity
of the blade in
my blunted being
my echoed screams

but here truly no
air to carry my
cry no dirt to root
no faces no
mutual breathing
or direction for
the tears that
cascade in my
helmet and dance—
intent amoebas
globule babes
with no down-
ward drift as they
rightly deserve

take me back
o I will connect

I promise! I will
find brothers
lover and kiss the
sere desert of
my O_2 solitude

abyss of blue
below is all I see
here and the promise
of a black vacuous
tarred god above

to float
might be
heaven but my
soul is still in
heavy hell
how I reel here
so reel me in
return me to
that sticky safe
bound ball
its coddling
mothering spin
to plant my heels
and spit glee

Thorazine Thoughts

Which is closer on the table— knife or pear?
The knife says *your urge to cut flesh is near.*
The pear responds *my seed is far,*
but my flesh close enough to bite if your
teeth can travel, if your tongue can bear.

Which is closer— meds or mountain?
Ice is nice, but can you climb my wall?
asks the mountain, *find my rapids to swim in.*
The meds say *we are magic as a fountain,*
but our lightness holds a ton of withdrawal.

Which is closer— heart or mind?
The heart says *I pump and love, pump and.*
The mind says *I'm at your ground zero,*
though I dream of "distance" and "long ago."

trilobite

come cambrian
child
out of this blooded
limestone
prison
come cryptic wild
unfossilized
from this tattered
coral
primordial
soup
and up
this
crepe
of a leg

do you lay
eggs
do you crawl
all
the intestinal
to have your
bottom-dweller
way?

19 Lines

It's the coming of attention deficit—
I can't read long poems anymore.
I thought it was something you were born with.

At about line 19 I think, this is it,
I'm done with this meandering one for
now. Perhaps it's the poem that has the deficit,

substanceless, or I'm not good at
getting the obscurity, the ghosted metaphor—
wow, you got me. But I have less patience with

other things too-- hearing a mouth
say more than a sentence or
two. Am I going deaf? Is it

the first rot of my wit?
When are we ready for the head to wear
out? Maybe my blossoming trouble with

anything long is like the death
of caring who is playing and what's the score
or the country's current deficit.
Is that something we were born with?

A Beautiful Goodbye

Take off your noose— more colorful ways to die.
It must be spangled, making you notorious,
a suicide that's easy on the eye.

You once chose razor— that one didn't fly—
blood reversed and clotted. You were furious.
Unknot the noose for colorful ways to die.

They say to live (oh, do you even try?),
unaware what brought it on, incurious.
Not seeing the cause is easy on their eye.

Something pushed you past all stimuli,
past bullied years till you were caged, delirious,
so dig for level-headed ways to die

or dream your expiration in the sky,
Vesuvian bright, no standard goriness.
One's death is easy to one's dreaming eye,

but ask yourself the simple question: why?
Go out with bang and rainbow if that's glorious—
but look for colorful reasons not to die,
a life cut short uneasy on the eye.

Autophile

I love my cars.
They're worth so much to me,
more than the stars.

I emptied my wife's purse,
looking for spare keys
to some of my classic cars

she thinks are hers.
The only wheels I see
in her future are bound for the stars—

a wide and beaten-up hearse,
that's all she was to me,
thinking she owned any of my cars,

and now she filed for divorce,
saying I wasn't a family,
that we weren't meant for the stars.

What's even worse,
she loved and raised my children for me
while I played with and loved my cars,
more than the stars.

Bedrock

Is this rock bottom?
We're a happy band of losers,
so smoke em if you got em

and be happy that the bedlam
above who called us boozers
is far from sweet rock bottom.

Let's just ignore them—
we can't sink any further,
so smoke em if you got em.

They're gloating on their totem,
every one of them a user.
Come visit rock bottom—

not many winners fathom
the loneliness we charter.
We smoke em when we got em,

and drinking is our demon,
but beggars can't be choosers
when you hit rock bottom,
so smoke em if you got em.

Cold Spell

You thought hell was other people,
but you made your hell alone—
cold space is torture,

no coming, no departure,
a single fork and spoon.
Where are all the people

who are loathing other people?
They are balls of huddled bone,
for sleeping can be torture,

no one there to nurture
a heart becoming stone
from fear of other people,

especially at a table
where others see your bones
to pick. It can be torture

to hear their warm laughter
and never hear your own,
thinking hell was other people,
but cold space is torture.

Losing Season

I'm losing.
My niece sent a card how much she loves me.
I felt nothing,

my heart receding,
dying quietly
from betrayals, cold shoulders, losing

lovers one too many times, wanting
to just go missing. *You, boy,*
said my father, *are nothing*

if you can't take the everyday prodding and using
by pinheads who think they
are anything but losing.

Maybe hell is other people, talking
down, causing nightmares till I gladly
want to be nothing,

and I hope my niece in all her love will be something,
not pared down, curled up the way
I am right now— losing,
feeling nothing.

My Raven

The dark around me isn't incidental—
a part of night has snared a part of me.
It's held me years, the feeling is substantial,

such that any reasoning's dismantled.
I shiver from a thing that I can't see,
a rap or thump that isn't incidental.

Perhaps a heart I broke is out to cripple
this life I've made, or some past enemy
knows my faults, my punishment substantial—

or so I think, imagination's tall
just like the beast I sensed when I was three
when closet creaks seemed more than incidental,

all dread deserved for being born so mental—
I never should have been allowed to breathe,
but terror gets me nowhere. I'm substantial

enough to know that fear is just a rental—
I'll give it back and place a stone in me
that dulls the edge of every incidence till
the aching that I live with less substantial.

Ouch

My brother hit me on the head with a bat.
I was maybe four, no, five.
The bump had red cracks, I paid for that,

staying small, dumb, nervous as a cat.
Since then I've never felt very alive—
sad, anxious, flighty as a bat,

close to drowning as a hurricane rat
in alcohol and sedatives—
my liver had red cracks, I paid for that

with no hunger and death close, I felt it,
but the fact I didn't want to live
had nothing to do with the blow of a bat.

I was an oddity and that's that,
born sensitive, emotionally massive,
full of wrath. I paid for that.

Being wack and flaked at
finding love breeds a soured fugitive.
My brother hit me on the head with a bat,
such red cracks, and I paid for that.

7

Learn the 7 deadly sins by heart,
though *deadly* is quite harsh, but never fuss—
observe their practice, imitating art.

Greed involves boldest strokes— impart
that wanting more requires vision. Trust
you'll learn the sin of vanity by heart—

insult a god and watch him burst apart.
The glutton— Rubenesque, he'll eat the best
of everything, even works of art.

The proud are proud that they are also art
that can't be touched.   All they do is just.
They know the 7 deadly sins, by heart.

Be mindful some destruction plays a part
to illustrate the reds of wrath and lust.
How envy grows, seeing the sins as art,

in those who never sin but burn to start.
Unfortunate, the ones who think they must
label acts to hide their soiled hearts,
who never know what is and isn't art.

Such A Piety

Joe is old, and God is getting close.
He made no plans for any pilgrimage
and can't decide which faith he loves the most.

They're all so different, he'll just be a host
to safe beliefs and saints that never age,
like God. Eternity is getting close,

so bless his soul he keeps a Christian house
where heathens would be christened in a cage—
he'd design a faith they love the most

till God decides what destiny is just:
such sacrifice to conquer sacrilege.
God's a cure, a lure, and getting close.

You could rip away Joe's Sunday clothes
and put him on a pedestal to judge—
he won't give in to men who hate him most

or live this life with aches he never chose—
he lived a book but could not turn the page
and overdosed when God was getting close.
In death he'll learn the faith God loves the most.

T

I can't make you love me, can I.
I can't reverse your heart,
and that's my end beginning for me.

I loved you to a T
walking towards me from the start,
but I can't make you love me, can I—

your anxious eye always in the sky
looking for higher hearts beside the stars,
and that's my end beginning for me—

the end of hoping I'd find somebody
searching equally, who wasn't too far
away to make them love me. Can I

breathe on while this love is close by?
Should I live and not love ever?
It's just my end beginning for me

as your new beginning is now ending me,
but I regret loving you, never!
I can't make you love me, can I,
and that's my end beginning for me.

The Swimmer

He came swimming
as I was sinking, a true life *guard*,
knowing I was running

out of time, pulling
me to shore without a word,
then asking why I was swimming

in currents surely funneling
to rock bottom so hard.
I said, *the river was running*

by so softly, and I was sunning,
when from the river I heard
the splash of people swimming—

kissing, drinking, and laughing,
and I became jealous. He said,
why, when you are running

a life so well on sand, staying
dry and level-minded, fed
love and literature? Swimming

in solitude leads to dying,
even on dry land. He stayed
a while till I wasn't running

out of breath, or lying
that I wouldn't go for dead
by again going swimming.

He said he was in pain, stemming
from his need to run, it led
to injury from running—

a red coal branding
inside his beaten leg. I read
another ache swimming

through his head, and something,
a similar drowning, flooding his head,
that, like me, left him running

in tired circles, finding
aim and drive gone bad,
only left with swimming

in water (and on land), seeming
fine but sharply sad,
and I knew life was running

fast for him, breeding
demons out for blood.
I'm thankful he came swimming

when I was drowning and being
stupid and afraid,
destructive and running

on booze, contemplating
a liquid suicide—
I'm glad, he too, was swimming

through a living barely breathing,
yet diving to my aid,
a pro at endless swimming,
though I know he'd rather be running.

The Poem Speaks

I am not a tragic poem—
just one without a sense of happiness,
in a world running out of room

for simple ennui in quiet homes
now occupied by jarring wealthiness
that no one writes a poem

about unless it tells how one may come
to such a state of careless bliss.
These are somber words— no room

for explanation or for whom
the bell will toll next , I guess
the best of times are here, with poems

serious and deep erased by some
who think that sorrow has no place,
that positivity fills rooms,

temporary till the tomb—
paralysis with snuffing space,
too cramped to write the least bit tragic poem
in a world running out of room.

Zag

Imagine a day when roughness is refined,
bedlam smoothed, no path pitted and bleak,
when time's reversal levels all mistakes
that etched our lives of mazes with no end.

Let reclination rule, and roars unwind—
with static gone, our shyness starts to speak,
revealing flaws and reasons we went weak.
Tired rifts inside begin to bind,

although unsteadiness goes on and on—
side to side we cling to piles of dirt,
or take to sky to keep from falling down

from aches in jolts and sanity unspun.
Crooked a god who never says a word
as tears stagger, never reach the ground.

Small-Minded

O
narrow-
eyed,
what do you see
when you see a vase with peony?

For I see a fist choked in glass,
the pounce of tenderness,
a mother calling children,
a squint of grieving face,
the wood nymph cauldron,
fireworks of flesh.

You see an eventual mess,
petals that disconnect.

Stevens was correct.
The world is ugly,
and the people are sad.

www.ingramcontent.com/pod-product-compliance
Lightning Source LLC
Chambersburg PA
CBHW050917220726
PP18604600002B/34